United We Stand

A Children's Patriotic Worship Experience

Created by Pam Andrews

Lillenas PUBLISHING COMPANY

Box 419527, Kansas City, MO 64141
lillenas.com

CONTENTS

We Are America 4
We Are America
You're a Grand Old Flag
Yankee Doodle Dandy

The Star-spangled Banner 21

My Country, 'Tis of Thee 25

America, the Beautiful 29

United We Stand *with* Battle Hymn of the Republic . . . 34

Production Notes 45

Clip Art 48

We Are America

with
You're a Grand Old Flag
Yankee Doodle Dandy

Words and Music by
PAM ANDREWS
Arranged by John M. DeVries

KID #1: We hold these Truths to be self-evident,
KID #2: ...that all Men are created equal,
KID #3: ...that they are endowed by their Creator with certain unalienable Rights,
KID #4: ...that among these are Life, Liberty, and the Pursuit of Happiness.

With pride ♩ = ca. 130

We're the U - nit - ed States of A-

*CD POINTS: Vocal Demo, CD:1; Split-channel, CD:6-16; Stereo Trax, CD:39

KID #1: We the people of the United States, in order to form a more perfect union,
KID #2: …establish justice, insure domestic tranquility, provide for the common defense,
KID #3: …promote the general welfare, and secure the blessings of liberty to ourselves and our posterity,
KID #4: …do ordain and establish this Constitution for the United States of America.

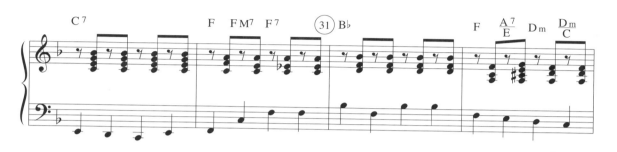

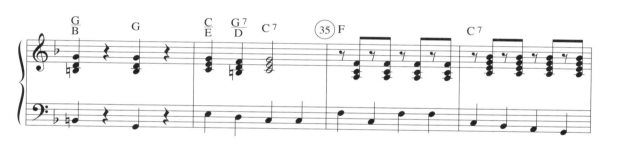

Faster ♩ = ca. 130
(Flag Corps enters marching down the aisle)

mer - i - ca, the brave and the true!

KID #1: Our flag is beautiful. The red and white stripes represent the 13
original colonies and the stars represent the 50 states.
KID #2: The colors of the flag have special meaning, too.
KID #3: The white stands for purity, the red for valor, and the blue for justice.
KID #4: Old Glory is an important part of our American heritage and should
always be held in honor.

12

KID #1: We should also honor our service men and women…
KID #2: …who have given so much to make our country great.
KID #3: These men and women have paid the price for our freedom.
KID #4: They have fought and died for you and me.

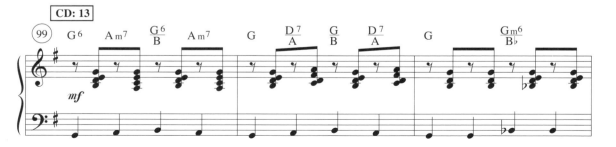

CD: 14

(Child in camouflage suit as if in the military marches center stage and salutes the flag)

109 *"Yankee Doodle Dandy"*

He's   a Yan-kee doo-dle dan — dy A Yan - kee doo-dle, do or

113

die;   A real live neph-ew of his Un - cle Sam,

CD: 15

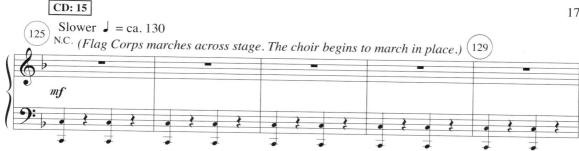

125 Slower ♩ = ca. 130

N.C. *(Flag Corps marches across stage. The choir begins to march in place.)* 129

mf

KID #1: Yes, we're America.
KID #2: The home of the free and the brave.
KID #3: And now more than ever…
KID #4: …we want to stand and say…

*Narration begins 133

CD: 16

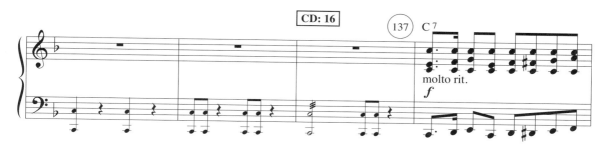

137 C7

molto rit.
f

f 139 accel.

We're the U - nit - ed States of A -

C7/G Gm7 C7 F

accel.

18

KID #1: Please stand for our pledge to the flag. *(drumroll begins) (Leads audience)* "I pledge allegiance to the Flag of the United States of America and to the Republic for which it stands, one nation under God, indivisible, with liberty and justice for all."

KID #1: The Star-spangled Banner was written by Francis Scott Key.

KID #2: It was written during the War of 1812.

KID #3: American Patriots were fighting for Independence and religious freedom.

KID #4: Key was aboard a British ship negotiating freedom for a prisoner of war when the British began bombing Fort McHenry.

KID #1: He waited through the night eight miles off-shore, praying that the fort would stand.

KID #2: To his joy, he saw with the dawn a giant American flag waving over the fort.

KID #3: He pulled an old letter from his pocket and wrote the words to our national anthem.

KID #4: Please join us in singing the Star Spangled Banner.

The Star-spangled Banner

FRANCIS SCOTT KEY

Attr. to JOHN STAFFORD SMITH
Arranged by John M. DeVries

*Music begins after the pledge of allegiance

*CD POINTS: Vocal Demo, CD:2; Split-channel, CD:17-20; Stereo Trax, CD:40

PLEASE NOTE: Copying of this product is NOT covered by CCLI licenses. For CCLI information call **1-800-234-2446.**

CD: 19

say, can you see, by the dawn's ear - ly light, What so

My Country, 'Tis of Thee

SAMUEL F. SMITH

Thesaurus Musicus
Arranged by John M. DeVries

KID #1: "America," also known as "My Country, 'Tis of Thee," was written by
Samuel Francis Smith, who was an outstanding young preacher and missionary.
KID #2: He wanted to write a patriotic hymn to inspire the people of his day.
KID #3: It was first performed by a children's choir led by Lowell Mason in Boston on
July fourth, 1833.
KID #4: The beauty of "America" is that it proclaims the leadership of God to our country.

With reverence ♩ = ca. 82

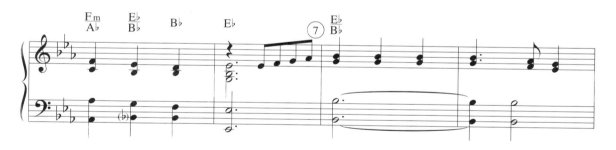

*CD POINTS: Vocal Demo, CD:3; Split-channel, CD:21-23; Stereo Trax, CD:41

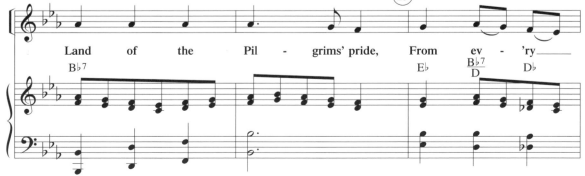

CD: 23

America, the Beautiful

KATHARINE LEE BATES

SAMUEL A. WARD
Arranged by John M. DeVries

KID #1: Katharine Lee Bates wrote one of the most famous patriotic hymns
 ever written.
KID #2: She was inspired to write this hymn while high atop Pikes Peak in Colorado,
 and also while visiting the World's Fair in an alabaster city, Chicago.
KID #3: She compared the beauty of God's nature with the creations of man.
KID #4: She ended each verse with a sincere prayer to God to lead us to do good.

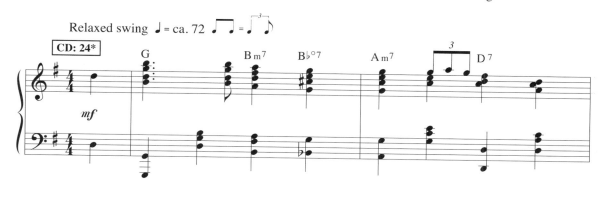

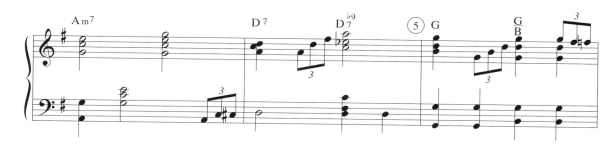

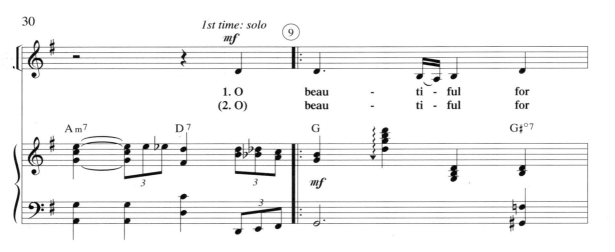

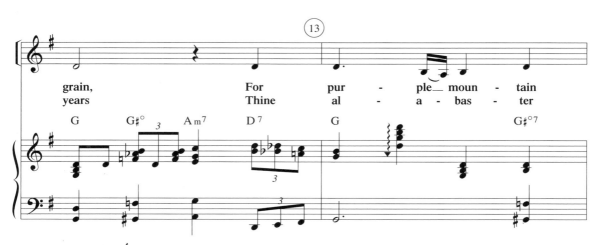

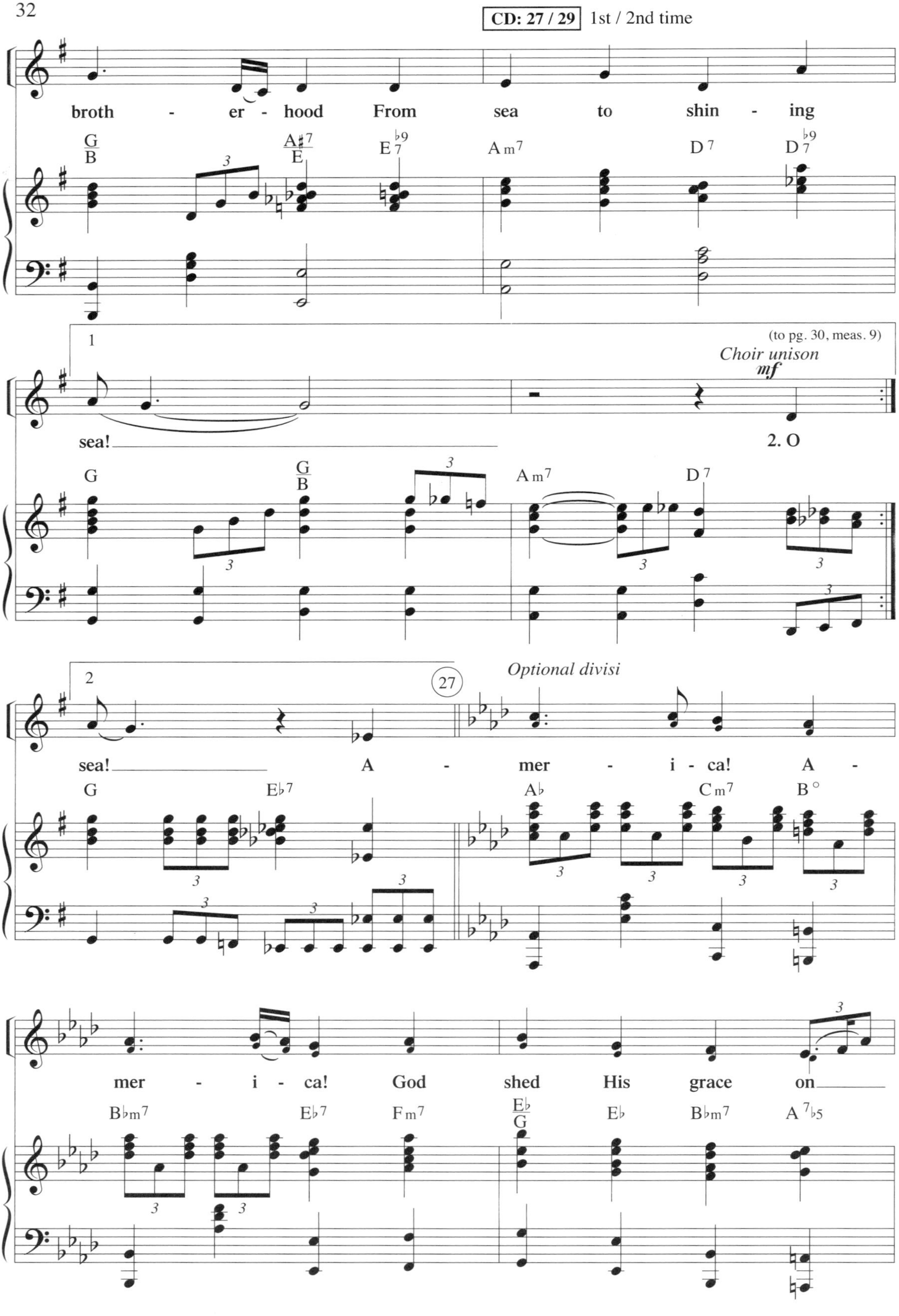

CD: 27 / 29
1st / 2nd time
broth - er - hood From sea to shin - ing
G/B A♯7/E E♭9 7 Am7 D7 D♭9 7
1
(to pg. 30, meas. 9)
Choir unison
mf
sea!
2. O
G G/B Am7 D7
2
27
Optional divisi
sea! A - mer - i - ca! A -
G E♭7 A♭ Cm7 B°
mer - i - ca! God shed His grace on
B♭m7 E♭7 Fm7 E♭/G E♭ B♭m7 A7♭5

United We Stand

with

Battle Hymn of the Republic

Words and Music by
PAM ANDREWS
Arranged by John M. DeVries

KID #1: Yes, we are Americans and we stand together in brotherhood. We were
founded on the principles of God. America's roots are found in Jesus
Christ. With Jesus we stand united.

ALL: United we stand!

KID #2: We are the soldiers of Christ spreading His good news of salvation all
across the world.

ALL: United we stand!

KID #3: We claim Jesus as our leader and we gladly follow His will.

ALL: United we stand!

KID #4: We stand united with Christ forevermore! His truth is marching on!

ALL: United we stand!

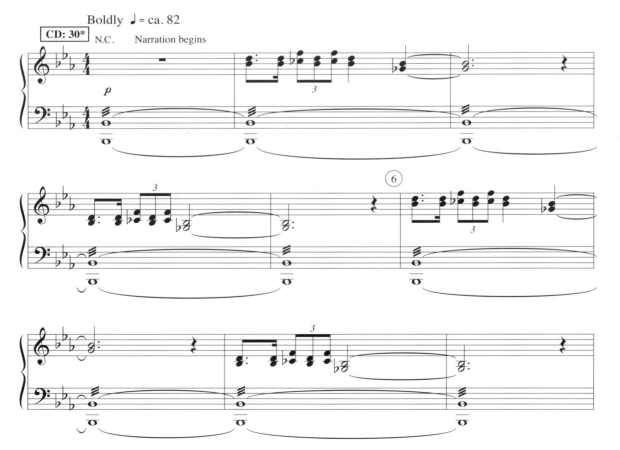

*CD POINTS: Vocal Demo, CD:5; Split-channel, CD:30-38; Stereo Trax, CD:43

CD: 32

Costumes

Choir	To accommodate the patriotic atmosphere, the children could wear blue jeans and white shirts with red or blue bandanas. They should have small American flags in their back pockets.
6 Flag Corp Members	The flag corp should dress the same as the choir but they should have red and blue ribbons draped from their left shoulder to their right waist front and back. Attach the ribbons at the waist with a small American Flag pin and allow for the ribbons to drape to the floor.
Boy Soldier	The boy soldier should wear camouflage clothing found at a local military store or department store.
Soldiers	They should dress the same as the boy soldier.
6 Fabric girls	They should red, white or blue turtlenecks which would match the color of the fabric they carry.

Optional Cast

Francis Scott Key	American Revolutionary style clothes
Samuel Francis Smith	Sports coat and Bible
Katharine Lee Bates	Lady in dress

Props

Small American Flags, 1 per child
U.S. Constitution
Large Bible
Red, White, and Blue sheer fabric 6 feet long

6 Large American Flags
Cross
Bible

Staging

These movements need to be coordinated with the section of the song below. "Dialogue" is as noted. Song lyrics are in italics.

<u>WE ARE AMERICA</u>
Opening Dialogue
> The choir should stand still. The speakers move to their microphones. Place two microphones stage right and two microphones stage left. The speakers remain at their microphones throughout the performance.

We're the United States of America... (measure 11)
> The choir should march in place.

Dialogue (page 7)
> The choir stands still. Have one child come forward holding the Constitiution.

America was founded... (measure 41)
> The choir remain still. Have one child come forward holding a large Bible.

We're the United States of America... (measure 51)
> The flag corp enters marching down the aisles to center stage. The choir marches in place.

Dialogue (page 11)
> The choir should march in place. They should get their flags from their pockets.

You're A Grand Ole Flag... (measure 83)
> The choir should march in place and wave their flags.

Dialogue (page 14)
> The choir should continue to march in place. A boy in camouflage suit marches to center stage and salutes the flag.

He's a Yankee Doodle Dandy... (measure 109)
> The soldier and choir marches in place. The flag corp moves next to the soldier with three flags on his left and three flags on his right.

Cadence section (measure 125)
> The choir should stand still.
> March forward 8 steps—reverse
> March back 8 steps—to the right
> March to the right 8 steps—reverse
> March to the left 8 steps—form a circle
> March in a circle 16 steps

Dialogue (page 17)

> The choir, soldier, and flag bearers march in place center stage. The flag corp marches across stage. The choir begins to perform a kick line waving their flags. They move into marching in place.

THE STAR-SPANGLED BANNER
Dialogue: Please stand for our pledge to the flag... (page 20)

> The speakers and choir all salute the flag while Kid 1 leads them and the audience in the Pledge to the flag. The speakers continue the dialogue while the choir continues to salute. Everyone, but the speakers move into the choir. Francis Scott Key moves center stage.

O say can you see by the dawn's early light... (measure 28)

> All stand at attention while saluting singing the "Star Spangled Banner." Francis Scott Key is center stage.

Dialogue (page 25)

> The speakers continue the dialogue. Francis Scott Key moves into choir. Samuel Francis Smith moves center stage.

MY COUNTRY, 'TIS OF THEE
My country,'tis of thee... (measure 15)

> Samuel Francis Smith stands stage right and the soloist for "America" moves to Kid 4 microphone.

Dialogue (page 29)

> The speakers continue the dialogue. Samuel Francis Smith moves into choir. Katharine Lee Bates moves stage left.

AMERICA, THE BEAUTIFUL
O beautiful for spacious skies,... (measure 9)

> During this song the fabric girls run across stage streaming the fabric behind. They can also gather the fabric and walk in circles. The solo for "America, the Beautiful" should sing at Kid 4 microphone.

UNITED WE STAND
Dialogue (page 34)

> This can be a responsive reading with the audience and choir.

Come, take my hand... (measure 14)

> A child holding the cross moves center stage. The choir holds hands.

Glory, glory... (measure 63)

> The choir walks forward holding hands. They raise their hands at the end of the song.

United
We
Stand

A Children's Patriotic Worship Experience

United We Stand

A Children's Patriotic Worship Experience

United
We
Stand

A Children's Patriotic Worship Experience

United We Stand

A Children's Patriotic Worship Experience

United
We
Stand

A Children's Patriotic Worship Experience